HAIKU ONE BREATHS

a voice through a tangle

D1593148

Allbook Books

written and edited, with calligraphy, by

Walter E. Harris III

Hauppauge, N.Y., U.S.A.

"Autumn (Oct. 8?) 1937"
From *Endless Vow* by Soen Nakagawa, translated by Kazuaki
Tanahashi and Roko Sherry Chayat. © 1996 by Eido Tai
Shimano, Kazuaki Tanahashi, and Roko Sherry Chayat.
Reprinted by arrangement with Shambhala Publications, Inc.,
Boston, www.shambhala.com

"Frisbees cut through clouds..." and "Lightning ignites sky..."
From *Spirits and Oxygen* by Yolanda Coulaz. Deposit, NY:
Purple Sage Press, © 2003 by Yolanda Coulaz, by permission
of the author/publisher.

Printed on recycled paper (85% recovered fiber /
30% post consumer) in the United States of America.

Published by: Allbook Books
               PO Box ~~14331~~ 562
               ~~Hauppauge, N.Y. 11788-0416~~
                           Selven, NY 11784

ISBN 0-9743603-1-7

COVER ART

The brush-calligraphy pictographs on the cover (sometimes called ideograms since they convey 'ideas' with pictures) are explained in depth in the introduction - Part 1, section 3.

Essentially, they transliterate to the book's title:

hai (top two) + **ku** (middle)
one (bottom – horizontal line)
breath (bottom – right)

and since **haiku** is both singular and plural..

haiku one breaths..
a voice through a tangle

Please Note:

Depending on your level of experience and knowledge, you can read this book from start to finish, or you can skip around. Structurally, however, the haiku poetry follows the information and suggestions so that you can better understand the poems as well as the techniques utilized.

with much thanks to:

- Richard for the book-size idea
- Jeanette for saying "get to work!" (more than once)
- Cliff for help with editing, suggestions, and being a fellow haiku friend and poet who espouses the true nature and integrity of the Art
- Barbara for her haiku sensibility and numerous haiku books
- George for prompting a fuller section on the applications of the haiku-essence to modern poetry
- Jeff for helping me to be sure that "haiku" is both singular and plural (though some do say "haikus")
- Yolanda for proofreading (notational 'quirks' and all..)
- Barbara, Jeanette and The Sagency for comments on the manuscript
- Singh for sea breezes
- Alan Watts for his inspirational calligraphy, scholarship, and truth-telling
- All the contributing poets for their fine haiku
- All those who gifted me with haiku books, encouraged the writing of this book, and shared their poems, feelings, ideas.. all of which have made this book, as well as my day to day life, a more pleasant and satisfying experience

the name

Allbook Books

honors   Uncle Alan

who was a kind man and a lover of books

"Nothing is little to him who feels it
with great sensibility."

-- Samuel Johnson

"The Way of Haiku requires not only a Franciscan
poverty, but this concentration of all the energies of
mind and body..."
-- R.H. Blyth *HAIKU, Vol. 1, Eastern Culture,* p. 294.

Of Zen's influence on haiku R.H. Blyth wrote:
"It is essentially a *wordless* state, in which
words are used, not to express anything,
but rather to clear away something that
seems to stand between us and the real
things which (in being not in fact separate
from ourselves) are then perceived by self-
knowledge."

-- *HAIKU, Vol. 1,* p.176.

introductory notes

Although this little book is mostly 'my work'.. the haiku of other dedicated haiku poets (as well as those just beginning or spontaneously haiku-ing now and then) have been added both to honor the work of some fellow poets and friends, as well as to give the entire book a larger 'voice' that reflects a 'community' of people and poets. The contributors' poems are identified by name, whereas, to avoid needless repetition, the un-named haiku are my work.

Although each haiku stands alone, the **haiku** sections have the flavor of *haikai-no-renga* "long linked-poem" from which *haiku* were derived.

*

While I have been enjoying reading and writing haiku over the past seven years, I hadn't planned to write a book about haiku. Rather, suddenly realizing I had enough of them for a book, I decided to make one, as well as to add an introduction on the somewhat elusive art of **how** to write them.

And so, I began examining my own process of writing haiku, and though this book is certainly not a complete explanation of such, the suggestions, basic guidelines, formulas and haiku examples do provide, I trust, a simple yet moderately detailed approach to the subject. Numerous other fine books provide additional and in-depth historical and technical information, so for those interested there is a bibliography with notes on what I feel each book adds to the subject (and there are many more books I haven't read). As with any creative process, keep in mind that, along with the basic common experiences of reading and writing haiku, you will find your own methods and nuances that facilitate yet another unique process and haiku experience.

What this little book has to offer is:
for the beginner— a creative primer along with brief mention of technical aspects of haiku.

for the intermediate— a refresher, along with specific haiku guidelines geared toward the process of writing and understanding haiku.

for the advanced— a fuller approach to the haiku process or haiku way of being.

For any level, this book offers (as far as I know) the only transliteration of the actual meaning of "haiku" as derived (albeit with some interpretation) from the original Chinese and modern Japanese *kanji* pictographs ('picture-symbols') or ideograms (ideas expressed with 'picture-symbols').

Even if you don't write poetry, by reading this book you will connect with the haiku consciousness which is really just another way of observing and experiencing the world.

Remember that, appreciation of the haiku art-form, as

well as being able to write quality haiku, requires *being in the moment*. How does one keep alert and in the moment when doing any task over and over? The title of a book by Shunryu Suzuki, *Zen Mind, Beginner's Mind,* gives one of the best answers I know of. As a beginner in anything, one pays special attention to learning. And so it is with life and haiku, for although one may have tons of experience, a certain amount of "beginner's mind" keeps one alert and responsive to the 'now.'

*

purpose

Along with encouraging the simple enjoyment of haiku.. this book is aimed at providing potential short-cuts to the understanding and writing of haiku. By short-cuts, I mean that one does not have to read every book on haiku before being able to write them well (though a bit of technical knowledge and insight helps). Although short-cuts can be helpful, one must also be careful not to overlook the essences and tech-niques that also assist haiku writing. The "short-cut" (which may take time to get to) is the 'state of being' from which most haiku inspirations occur. Editing and polishing 'the poem' is typically a second phase.

This book has some technical information yet is pri-marily focused on the creative process. I try not to memorize specific 'how-to' techniques so as to culti-vate more of the 'original voice' or "beginner's mind" and so allow the experience to 'speak through me.' For example, one can go looking for haiku contrast in nature: *the huge cloud / the tiny bug...* but I find these attempts to have a bit more forced or intellectual taste, whereas if I were to *spontaneously* see a huge cloud and tiny bug somehow connected there would be more 'realism' in the haiku.

You can memorize techniques and yet not walk around trying too hard to fit the haiku experience and subsequent poem into a category. After the purity of the intitial impulse of the haiku moment occurs, you can apply some of the techniques to see if they help the haiku take shape.

Try various methods and see. Without forcing numerous 'prescriptions' you may write fewer haiku at first, but you will be cultivating a haiku-awareness that will change your perceptions and help you to write more and better quality haiku in the long run.

The topic of applying the haiku experience to more imaginative and longer poems is dealt with toward the end of this book.

*

one breaths of haiku are...

heightened or subtle moments of awareness;

word-pictures;

poetic-short-speak;

AHA! revelation;

AHH-ness;

significant moment;

'nothing special' moment;

humorous or quirky phrase;

bird-sounds;

mantra;

poetic riddles;

simple communications;

a deep breath of fresh air;

something to Be With and Contemplate

the Experience and 'Teaching' of the poem;

an impersonal phrase, sentence, or verse;

'a way or voice through a tangle'..

expressed through the shortest of poetic forms..

a gift from Japan..

haiku

"...in a haiku moment of one breath-length,

there is only the resolution." -- Kenneth Yasuda

The Japanese Haiku, p.61.

contemplation

(note: Since Japanese *kanji,* or picture-writing, is derived from ancient Chinese, I have chosen ancient Chinese pictographs/ideograms to represent a central concept to this book.

excercise: Look at the ancient Chinese pictographs and contemplate:
1) Left Side – (horizontal line):
    the one-ness of being; primordial unity;
    the source
2) Right Side – the Breath (curvy line)..
    moving through an Obstacle (horizontal line)..
    and ultimately Breathing Freely
    (small upper horizontal line)
3) the pictograph as a whole

Doing this can enable one to become serene, as well as aware of the calming and energizing nature of One Breath.. and another Breath.. and One Breath...

The pictograph can also serve as a 'place of reference' for calming and focusing your energies, thoughts, emotions, etc. This may or may not help you write haiku, but it will connect you with another level of being and thus enhance your well-being.. and perhaps put you in that place of receptivity that is essential for haiku.

The pictograph of what a haiku is trans-literally.. will be explored later on.

contents

"...*haiku* is a pebble thrown into the pool of the
listener's mind, evoking associations out of the
richness of his own memory. It invites the listener
to participate instead of leaving him dumb with
admiration while the poet shows off."
— Alan Watts *The Way of Zen* pp.183-84.

*

Part 1 - Structure and Technique

cultural overview

Haiku are poetic-literary expressions from a culture that values humility, precision, and a connection with the true nature of being (or Spirit) through daily ritual. Although not limited to Zen, haiku is considered one of many Zen Arts. Others are: Tea ceremonies *cha-no-yu* "the art of tea," and *chado* "the way of tea"; *kodo* (incense ceremony); Zen rock gardens; *feng shui* "wind-water" (the art of placement and natural energy flow); *ikebana* "the art of flower arranging"; *shakuhachi,* the hollow, Zen flute; *sumi-e* painting and brush calligraphy; *kendo* "the way of the sword"; the classic *Noh* Theater; and the martial arts of which *tai chi chuan* (Chinese) is the most peaceful— all forms whose 'products' are visibly sparse, yet whose inner workings are quite vast.

Many of these Arts (along with Zen *koans* or Master-pupil interchanges) are classified by some as belonging to the Rinzai school of Zen which aims toward 'sudden recognition or enlightenment,' as compared with the Soto school whose aim is a gradual moving toward such a state of awareness, or more like 'there is no where to get to' Buddhist approach. Both of these qualities are apparent with haiku.

Haiku have the smooth timelessness of tai chi; the brushstroke motions of sumi-e painting or calligraphy; the natural precision of flower arranging; the grace of a tea ceremony; the mask of Noh theater; the austere beauty of a rock garden; the immediacy of a sword; the positive energy-flow of feng shui.

haiku overview

Haiku are a creative offshoot of and reflect the spiritual traditions and philosophies of, especially, Buddhism (more specifically Mahayana Buddhism,) Taoism, Zen and Zen Buddhism where the emphasis is taken off of the mere ego-self, thus allowing one to better experience the 'other' and Greater parts of Self. However, please note that classical haiku poems are not of themselves precepts nor necessarily any of the direct teachings of those enlightened philosophies and spiritual practices; haiku may reiterate such principles, or reflect the essence of such, but any similarities as well as differences need to be honored. There are numerous literary infuences as well, among them are Buddhist and Chinese poetry. Although lacking descriptive language, haiku exemplify a literary cell, a building-block of larger literary molecular structures.

Haiku's popularity outside of Japan is a kind of gift that resulted from WW II, for it was while R.H. Blyth (tutor to Crown Prince Akihito,) Harold G. Henderson, and Faubion Bowers were stationed in Japan that they learned of haiku in great depth. Kenneth Yasuda (Shôson) is also an influential haiku figure, and the writings of D.T. Suzuki and Alan Watts helped familiarize the West with Asian culture, arts, and philosophy.

With their various writings and encouragement, haiku have flourished and become easily recognizable as well as very popular. Ezra Pound dabbled with the form, as did Wallace Stevens and others, but 'beat'

poets Jack Kerouac and Gary Snyder helped to pop-
ularize the form in 'layman's' language. From elementary
school to the elders.. haiku are now enjoyed worldwide!

Encouraging cultural exchanges might actually help to
prevent wars.

*

This book is a blend of **haiku** (which traditionally require
some reference to nature and typically a "season-word"
(kigo) that identifies the season, as well as a
"cutting-word" (*kireji*) or pause within the poem; **senryu**
(which tend to highlight the human element and are
often more satirical and ironic, than humorous); and
what could be called **aphorisms**, **adages, or pithy
statements** that utilize the basic haiku structure..
though little else.

While varying poets, societies, and haiku aficionados
give varying definitions of what a haiku is, I personally
consider all of these poems as 'haiku', or more specifically: American, English-language haiku. Some call them
Western haiku (as Jack Kerouac did,) North American
haiku, or even Ameri-ku, and then there are worldwide
haiku in various languages plus some from poets that
write and speak English, though they are not American.

Along with being poems, haiku and the experience of
reading and writing them are, for some, a way of life.

*

haiku tool-kit

Some prefer to write longhand or on computers, or record their spoken words, yet a haiku poet's tool-kit can be as simple as: a pocket notebook, pad, Post-It notepad.. and pen or pencil. On occasion I have awakened from a dream to record a haiku, and so keep pen and paper handy (also for dreams).

*

artistic perspective

Like numerous Asian landscape paintings where the people are a mere speck on the scene, haiku are miniscule moments on a literary canvas.. but not necessarily any less valid or inspiring.

*

1
basic structure

While there is a wide scope of what a haiku is, the 'purer' ones drawing on the classical Japanese style (with room for contemporary innovations) have:

1) some reference to nature, or nature and human nature interacting

2) (more specifically) a "season-word" *kigo*, and if not, a "keyword"

3) have an internal pause, or "cutting-word" *kireji*

4) do not 'explain' or over-describe

5) rarely use simile; use metaphor subtly, if at all

6) convey the actual experience with as few words as possible

7) have an "aha!" or "ahhh..." quality
8) have a sense of immediacy

Attention to this list honors the traditional/classical origins while also allowing room for innovation.

Considering that a vast number of people on the planet live in urban and even suburban environments, does that make them any less apt to write haiku? Although I have no statistics on the subject, I would say "no," for the haiku sentiment or way of life, though it connects with nature, is first and foremost a 'state of being' available to anyone, anywhere. Parks, patios, porches, even that lone tree on a city block are all fodder for haiku. Urban haiku poetry would tend to reflect the setting, yet the essence of haiku is the key.

> Pigeons flying
> up the avenue--
> rush-hour traffic

One day at a busy suburban stoplight (with left and right turn signals) I saw a starling on a wire, and the bird's serenity and stillness prompted me to write:

> car traffic muffled,
> on a telephone wire
> starling unruffled

While rhyme is generally frowned upon in haiku, if used effectively, I find it adds a pleasant touch as well as making the little poem even easier to remember.. like a mini adult nursery rhyme.

*

the 'nature' of haiku
Haiku is sometimes defined as "humorous stanza" or "playful verse," though Matsuo Bashô (considered the Shakespeare of haiku) lifted the art to have greater meaning.

Much of the modern English emphasis has been on nature only. However, the differentiating between nature, human, and humor seems rather arbitrary to me. In fact, I couldn't count the number of times that 'nature' (and specifically the creatures that inhabit that domain) has made me smile and laugh. See that squirrel finding his way from tree to tree? That dog walking its owner? Me stepping right into that rainy day puddle?

While the nature element is traditionally accepted as a part of haiku and essential for 'grounding' the poem in the 'real world,' I feel that much of modern haiku has been reduced to an over-emphasis on ONLY nature, often resulting in bland word-pictures that are, in my opinion, barely haiku. Here is a made-up one as an example:

the autumn tree
and all its colors
the blue sky

Pretty as a picture, but this is a barely ok haiku image, lacking the "AHH... that's beautiful" or the "AHA! that's a high moment" or anything unusual. One can rather easily jot down impressions or observations in a haiku-like manner, but the leap, as it were, to 'haiku consciousness' and thus perception and expression, is some of what this book is about (i.e. the short-cut).

Even after reading numerous well-crafted 'nature' haiku I find myself craving a little something more. Although humor is considered by many as an element of *senryu*, it is my desire/feeling that 'natural humor' become more a part of modern haiku. Read the classics as well as the variety of contemporary haiku and label for yourself the variety of moods, topics, and so forth.

R. H. Blyth, in his *HAIKU* (4 volume work) identifies 7 main categories of haiku and organizes the haiku accordingly (mostly for organizational purposes,) and they are by no means restrictive categories. Among these are two that I feel have been overlooked by many modern haiku poets: 1) "Temples and Shrines: This is called in Japanese, Gods and Buddhas." This includes festivals, pilgrimages, and the visiting of graves (as the culture has deep respect for the ancestors). (Vol 1, p.338.)

This category is the slimmest and yet the question arises: is Western culture so sparse with "gods" and enlightened beings? Modern American haiku do mention Christmas and other holidays, yet the same sense of reverence for the "gods" and those of Buddha-stature is lacking. Christ is quoted as speaking in zen-like riddles, a la 'easier for a camel to go through the eye of a needle than for a rich man to get to heaven,' yet somehow what he represents is scant in haiku. For any poet of any spiritual tradition or combination thereof, one's "gods," Angels, Archangels, Saints, holy people, nature spirits, etc. are all potential reverential 'subjects' for haiku.

The other category is "Human Affairs: In Japanese "the things of men." It deals with the change of clothes, fishing, secular activities, rice-planting, fireworks, scarecrows, etc."(p.338). Again, though modern haiku highlight many of man's day-to-day and mundane activities, somehow this category has been considered secondary to Nature. However, all is connected and the reason one puts on a pair of wool socks or tank-top is inevitably due to the weather, and hence one's natural surroundings.

As well, are not the professions of 'mechanic,' 'food-service worker,' 'truck driver' and so on, every bit as valuable? Of course they are!

The other five categories listed are: 1) The Seasons; 2) The Sky and Elements; 3) Fields and Mountains...in

Japanese, geography. It comprises rivers, the sea, mountains, moors, paddy-fields; 4) Birds and Beasts; 5) Trees and Flowers: In Japanese, botany. It includes turnips, leeks, mushrooms and so on. (p.338).

The humorous element of haiku tends to reflect the humor of life with a flavor the Japanese call *karumi,* "lightness". Haiku often utilizes puns and word-play, rather than jokes or put-downs.

*

haiku sounds and syllables

I prefer not to be overly concerned with 'proper' syllable counts, instead allowing the poetic moment to speak for itself in whatever form suits it best. Some of these haiku poems read as 5-7-5 syallable count, yet most do not. Some even rhyme (mostly subtly,) though most do not.

9-12 syllables is considered by many as equivalent to the *onji* "sound-symbols" of Japanese language. Another approach is 2/3/2 'beats' or 'stresses,' rather than sylla-bles.

Although these loose definitions may seem to promote writing just about anything and calling it a haiku, that is not how I approach the process. There are many guide-lines and 'rules' from traditional Japanese haiku (and their adaptations to another language) that do help with the writing of American, English-Language haiku.

loose definition: 3 lines, typically short/long/short of 9 to 17 syllables (though I have read translations that are over 20 syllables and modern haiku of only 2 syllables). "Loose" allows for the syllables and the small percentage of haiku that I've seen that are 1 line with spacing between phrases; 2 lines; 4 lines, or more. (For the most part, Japanese haiku are actually written in one vertical line.) "Loose" also allows for line-length variations: long/short/short; short/short/long; long/short/long; etc. all depending on what best suits the purpose.. for it is the expression of the 'haiku essence' that is the key. The most familiar looking haiku is still: short/long/short.

As poet and critic Gary Corseri aptly states about the creative process and following specific forms while also allowing for a bit of leeway:

"Inspiration finds its own form."

*

inspiration & the creative process
(now to the actual experience of writing haiku)
While occasionally a haiku may be 'well-crafted,' I find that the best or purest ones happen spontaneously.. when one is receptive to the beauty, mystery, wonder, and such-ness of the moment or experience.. then **being able to convey the actual experience (with as few words as possible) exactly as it occurred.**
(One friend of mine wrote a bunch of haiku about past experiences, but the recollections were so vivid and 'in the moment' that they work. So you see, there are

10

basic guidelines, but absolutes will not serve us in the realm of haiku and the creative process. For some, writing haiku is a more deliberate process.)

As a journal excercise, at the end of the day one could contemplate the day's highlights and write a haiku. Although one step removed from the 'in the moment' format, this can make for nice poems cultivating haiku consciousness, and at the least, a way of journaling for the over-busy or those who like to be succinct:

> blue jay at dawn
> warmth of dinner with friends
> quick autumn sundown

Granted, perceptions can be subjective, yet haiku predominantly aim for an objective, non-personal form of expression. This does not exclude references to people or one's self but does point at minimizing any self-importance.

*

Here are some basic formulas that complement the "8 basic structure" list. (Some of the formulas naturally overlap, and you'll probably find more on your own. You can read and practice one at a time, and/or read them all first.)

formula (1)
levels of awareness

A blend of spontaneous **heightened** and/or **subtle** awareness AND the words to express that.. along with a bit of understanding of the form and 'craft' (which is especially handy when editing that initial impulse or creative moment,) is a nice formula for enhancing one's own appreciation for, and writing of, this lovely little poetic form. (Please re-read this.. several times!)

(MEMORIZE: A blend of spontaneous **heightened** and/or **subtle** awareness AND the words to express that!)

What that 'place' of heightened or subtle awareness of a haiku moments is.. you can explore and discover for yourself. I find that a certain 'empty-mindedness' (or Zen *wu-hsin* "no-mind" or *wu-nien* "no-thought",) while keeping all the senses alert, allows me to notice such moments. This 'empty-mind' is not 'stupid,' rather, not clouded with mental confusion.

Or, sometimes just happening to notice something unusual or cosmically ironic--

> homeless man gazing
> through the restaurant window--
> fall birthday dinner

Although this might be classified as a *senryu* for its highly human (though not humorous) subject matter, the 'heightened awareness' of that moment, along with the 'subtlety' of noticing the moment, created a certain energy-surge that (in my experience) signals "haiku!" "senryu!" "significant moment!" "write this down!"

I was having a birthday dinner with my family at a cof-feeshop when, suddenly, a scruffily dressed man (prob-ably homeless) looked in the window at the table, and I said, "that is a haiku moment!" Later on, while reflecting on the experience, the haiku was actually written. The haiku moment started when the man looked through the window. I put the "birthday dinner" at the end to convey the surprise and emotion I felt.

So the point is: be aware of what it is about the situation or moment that prompts the haiku and convey that with words.

After many months, I decided to add the word "fall" (it was late September) so as to have a "season-word" and make this more of a haiku. After doing so, I realized that the mention of season adds an extra element of reality, as well as compassion for the 'homeless man.'

formula (2)
recognition/sensory surges; don't try to write haiku
This is not just reverse psychology. For recognizing that a haiku is 'happening,' I normally notice/experience that there is a combination of (one or more of) seeing, hearing, smelling, tasting, touching, along with a clear awareness, all combined with a **'surge'** of

energy/feeling/emotion that says: **'this is noteworthy!'**

Alan Semerdjian describes the process as "similar to picking grapes off a leaf, fruit off a tree."

For me it is the moment of biting into the fruit, though one could consider THAT as the sharing of the haiku. Suffice it to say: haiku is "a ripe moment."

The process is: "Organic. When something strikes me in an emotional way, words seem to appear," according to Saul Waring.

Cliff Bleidner, a Zen-practitioner with twenty years of haiku experience, says that a haiku poet is a "trained observer," thus trained to recognize the haiku moment or experience. He describes the haiku essence as (non-violently) "three bold strokes with a sword."

Vivina Ciolli knows she has a completed haiku when the following criteria are met: "My 'tests' are: if I can read the poem slowly, knowing more as I move along the poem one word at a time; if there is no word or punctuation or spacing I 'must' change; and if the hair on my neck stands, each time I read it."

Kay J. Wight writes: "I have not been able to sit and plan to write a haiku... for me it has to be a moment, a sound, a smell, or just casting an eye on something that inspires me to want to paint or write or somehow capture the "feeling" so that I might share with others."

On a frigid winter night with high winds, I made some toast, and the orange glow from the toaster coils was visually 'noteworthy' along with the little bit of warmth it provided. This spontaneously contrasted nicely with the cold, windy weather:

> orange glow
> from the old toaster—
> 30 mph winds

This formula is also: "don't try to write haiku," simply observe and feel, and learn to recognize what is a haiku moment or experience worth jotting down; or sometimes the words are just *there* and pop out.

Following this formula I have sometimes gone for months without writing a haiku, and then suddenly 3 or 5 may occur in a week. Yet everyday I read at least one haiku of other writers, some classical, some modern.. so there is still that connection with the **haiku essence**.

formula (3)
sequential or time-lapse moments

While some haiku happen 'all at once' as a whole momentary experience of stirring significance, others happen sequentially (though the reader may not be able to tell the difference). For example:

out of nowhere
your friendly phone call—
big, gentle snowflakes

I received a pleasant surprise phone call. After the call a few minutes transpired, then I went outside and saw a few large snowflakes coming down.. thought about the phone call, and THEN the two experiences 'connected' to form the haiku. Both the call and the snowflakes had an 'out of nowhere' quality that linked them, unintentionally, together.

formula (4)
time-frame or story-line

Although the inspiration may happen in a flash, some haiku convey a story-line or cover a longer period of time, and generally leave a lot for the reader to ponder or fill in the blanks.

early people catch
the sunlight; or sleep late
catch the moonlight

-- Kay J. Wight

(This could easily read as a couplet, but here is a case where the line-breaks and enjambment enhance the rhythm and highlight the word "catch.")

formula (5)
invoking the spirits

"My personal theory, not especially well-informed, about *kigo* is that their origin is shamanic, animist, and ritualistic, that the words for "winter blast" and "spring blossoms" and "summer shower" were intended at one time to call forth the living spirits manifested in those natural phenomena."

(Robert Hass *The Essential Haiku* p.314.)

While haiku writing might appear to be simply a receptive art (i.e. allowing outside stimuli to inspire one,) I like Hass' theory because one can approach haiku writing as a kind of shaman who must respect the natural surroundings as well as provide ritualistic invocations and blessings for his/her people.

As American Indians and other tribal peoples (such as the Inuit) offer prayers to the spirits of animals they catch for food, or (the Hopi) give prayers and thanks to the 'corn maiden,' so too perhaps the haiku poets "call forth the living spirits manifested in those natural phenomena."

White footsteps—
in deep snow a clean path
for the world.

-- Sheila Mardenfeld

(This has a metaphorical quality, and yet, since what each individual does somehow affects the world as a whole, this haiku can be read literally as, 'my footsteps in snow are an example of a clean path for the world.')

formula (6)
catalogue of records & guidance; blessings.
(ok.. try to write haiku)

cataloguing/recording:
Look for haiku!

What is unique about today? The yellow forsythia petals faded just as the rose bush started blooming; first day of school; summer downpour of rain just after the car wash! Migratory patterns of birds. Sunlight or moonlight lighting a particular place at a particular angle on a specific day of the year, a la Stonehenge. Any significant moments? Or even some world-event co-incidence:

chaos in Iraq
tornadoes batter the midwest--
spring day

*

guidance
Write and record as if you are leaving a garden, yard or seasonal guidebook to a future resident or to a traveler so they know what to look for and when. Or simply a yearly calendar:

> mid-May
> he's from out of town
> oriole whistling

blessings
Have a sense of participating with nature and the environment, and, through your haiku, provide blessings.

> Miles Davis' trumpet,
> the ice cream truck's jingle--
> one fine June day

formula (7)
relating with others
simple communications & *renku* (or *renga*)
Kenneth Yasuda attributes the "Pre-Haiku Period" to the brief "...greetings exchanged by the deities Izanagi and Izanami at their first meeting..." (*The Japanese Haiku* p.109.)

Before haiku, perhaps brief poetic interchanges between people were often conversational (even intimate,) and being the length of what one can speak with one breath this may have heightened the level and respect for daily greetings and chit-chat. "Hello" and "how are you?" and "lovely day" are the little phrases we often share. By adding a little color to these phrases, we begin to actually **speak** with haiku-language:

> "beautiful sunrise
> the air so fresh and clean
> pleasant day to you."

This might not be the best haiku, but if a stranger said that to you while walking past you on the street, I'm quite sure that your mood would be lifted.. possibly for the entire day!

Perhaps originally haiku were also significant or life-altering comments of only a few well-said and poetic words.. from Teacher to Student, Master to Pupil, Parent to Child, person to person, deity to deity, deity to person, bird to person, and so on...

The following began as a haiku to which Ellen Blickman responded forming a "linked-verse," and since this only has one link, it is in *tanka* form (which can also be written by one person). The longer, linked form is *haikai-no-renga*, from which the solitary *haiku* is derived. (More about that later.)

> What are you feeling spider?
> Your web keeps bending
> with this autumn wind.

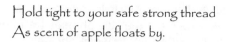

Hold tight to your safe strong thread
As scent of apple floats by.

The way this poem started fits a category of **talking to or addressing nature** and helps to connect one with childlike wonder. "Why is the sky blue?" "Rabbit, are you hungry at night?" "Do I seem huge to you, ants?"

Issa, one of the haiku Masters, is renowned for his compassion for the little ones.

formula summary

You can pick one "formula" and try that for a week, or combine elements of several at once. See what works for you, but do be aware of the various methods as that will help you to cultivate your own haiku sensibilities.

For a while (when especially busy with other writing projects) I only wrote what came to me spontaneously. Then, when I started to devote more time to haiku, I decided to try to write one each day, but without forcing poorly written haiku to happen. (One a day is a lot, but my natural output did increase.)

As a beginner, pushing a bit may help you to discover the purer ones from the forced. Or, you may decide to take a more contemplative route and let the haiku come to you. Explore.. and see what works.. for you!

Whatever the case, noting what inspires you, or moves

you to jot down such moments is a step toward discovering your own way to, and means of, writing and speaking haiku. Phrases or notes jotted down, just about anywhere, may be the seeds of a future haiku moment, spontaneous or otherwise.

With a little practice it becomes more familiar. And even if you don't create what some others may call 'real haiku'.. so what! At least you are cultivating a manner of recording moments and experiences that are special or important enough to remember. Besides, there are various schools and definitions about what makes a haiku, and you might just be the one to add some new flavor to the form.

Anyone can write haiku, though normally it takes a little while to sharpen your skills enough to write the ones that have that extra little "AHA!" or "AHHH..." feeling.

*

2
haiku as part of life (literary and otherwise)
Haiku can be used for:
- honing writing skills (editing for precise word choices)
- recording precious moments
- charting the seasons
- experiencing the subtleties of nature
- entering into a higher level of perception and
  consciousness.. thus in turn, enhancing one's
  appreciation of life's experiences.

Haiku are sometimes uneventful and bland, yet some may only seem so because you are not reading it at a moment that is pertinent to your current life experiences, or perhaps simply because that particular haiku (like a fruit or vegetable) is out of season.

Having already mentioned some basic experiential guidelines, let's look at some of the key traditional flavors that honor the haiku origins and so influence modern haiku. Traditionally, Japanese haiku have a "**season-word**" (*kigo*). Cherry blossoms in Japan (along with numerous other references) equal springtime.. so writing 'cherry blossoms' automatically lets the reader know what season it is in the poem, and perhaps even what week if the phase of a blossom is mentioned, or what day if a holiday (like Buddha's birthday) is mentioned. This is akin to various American Indian tribes having names for each full moon, as in "strawberry moon," or the Westernized "harvest moon."

"For example, "full moon" indicates, unless expressed otherwise, the full moon of the harvest—that is, the finest example of full moon to be had each year. And so, "full moon" is a season word for autumn, even though full moons certainly occur other times during the year." (Jim Kacian "First Thoughts -- A Haiku Primer" <http://blogs.law.harvard.edu/ethicalesq/stories/ storyReader$1352> 7 July 2004.)

The traditional Japanese "season-words" are highly specific and because they reflect localities, readers outside the 'province' just won't get them. Therefore, a "seasonal feeling" suffices for much modern and even non-Japanese haiku. "Animism" is the root of "season-words," according to Ban´ya Natsuishi. He also encourages "keywords" which encompass both "season-words" and **"non-season words" (muki)**. Thus, there are gradations of seasonal specifics, generalities, and none at all. ("Technique used in Modern Japanese Haiku" by Ban´ya Natsuishi <http://www.worldhaiku.net /archive/natsuishi1.html> 4 Aug 2004.)

While many modern English-language haiku do not utilize a season-word, I find that it is something worth paying attention to when writing. In a highly technological world (and specifically the American culture) where Labor Day, Memorial Day, a back-to-school sale, and the first baseball pitch signal the seasons-- a stronger connection to nature and its cycles would certainly help with the preserving of the beauties of this lovely planet that gives so much to us.

And for the reader, season-words highlight points in time each year and thus help one to further appreciate such moments. I often find myself looking to haiku that I have written (arranged by date) to determine if this year's first snow or first bird sighting coincides with the previous years.

> May sunshine--
> now all those winter months
> just memory

This was a moment in spring that (for me at least) signalled a 'healing' moment or a letting go of winter's struggle on a sensory level. And those are the kinds of moments I like to record and remember as part of my life-journey, for it keeps me attentive: when and where and who will I be with at that 'moment' in autumn when I notice that the warm weather has decidedly shifted? I also record the date of each of my haiku.

The more precise the moment, the more precise the season-word. There may be a particular day in spring when the majority of leaves have unfurled, or a particular week when a certain bird returns to your yard. Being a bit of a scientist here helps make your haiku much sharper and more accurate nature-wise.

Many traditional haiku have lines like "spring rain" and "autumn wind." So, while many season-words are subtler, sometimes it simply is appropriate to write "winter" or "spring".. and fill in the blank if necessary.

An alternative to "season-words" are "keywords": "The most useful way of thinking of the idea of keywords is not as a one-to-one replacement for *kigo*, but rather as an overarching system of correspondences available to the haiku poet which incorporates *kigo* within its bounds."

    (Jim Kacian "Beyond Kigo: Haiku in the Next Millennium" First Published in *In Due Season: Acorn Supplement #1* [2000] <http://www.iyume.com/kacian/beyondkigo.html> 6 July 2004.)

Kacian distinguishes the "seasonal feeling" of a key-word from the very specific association of most season-words.

The "keyword" method has also been written about by Ban´ya Natsuishi, a Japanese haiku poet, in essays and his *Keyword Dictionary* (ki-wa-do jiten, 1990.) The extensive Japanese listing of *kigo* and their associations have been best approached in English by William J. Higginson.

As each season begins and ends, a time of heightened seasonal shifts.. the haiku poet would be wise to pay special attention to *kikan* "seasonal feeling."

*

reading and writing tip
Since haiku are so short, an oral tradition among some modern haiku poets who read their work aloud is to read the poem twice. This enables the reader to hear the poem with two different inflections or emphases and also allows the listener to understand more deeply. As well, when reading haiku on a page, reading them at least twice allows the reader to go deeper into the poem and understand its various subtleties.

*

2 basic ways to read haiku
You could read an entire book of haiku in a short time, picking out your instant favorites, AND YET to get a fuller experience, reading haiku requires the reader to slow down, pause, savor the moment.. read slowly,

contemplate, see where the poem takes you and what you may have to figure out to better understand.

The *kireji* or "cutting-word, pause, caesura," also points out a place within the haiku where a natural pause occurs (this mentioned in detail later on). There are some variations of this, such as "pillow words" and "pivot words."

Those are (however briefly explained) the structural and practical basics. Now, a look at the inner state of the craft and technique of haiku.

*

editing
Here's one example of the editing process. The initial inspiration and ability to write a few words happened while in a car.. then a few edits at home.

> stuck in traffic
> almost napping until
> a bee flies in

> stuck in traffic
> nearly napping until
> a bee flies in

> stuck -- humid traffic,
> nearly napping until
>   the bee flies in!

The initial impulse is the same, but "stuck --" appropriately slows the poem down; and "humid" is more specific. (Typically this would indicate mid-to-late summer, although with so-called global warming, who knows?.. as this was written in spring. In this case it doesn't matter much.) Also, "the bee" because there's more personality than generic "a bee"

I suppose this could also read as:

    stuck -- humid traffic, nearly napping until
        the bee flies in!

or

    stuck--
    humid traffic, nearly napping until
        the   flies
            bee   in!

Ah! the possibilities...

I find that sometimes the haiku come through pure.. other times a few edits over time are needed. Basic editing procedures for poetry apply here as well. Pay attention to sound and rhythm, punctuation, capital letters, and so on, as well as the image itself and all that the haiku evokes, especially the 'mood.' Kenneth Yasuda advises looking at a haiku a bit like a journal-ist, so as to know the "when, where, and what." Also, re-read to see if the poem, as a whole, expresses or sees into the 'true nature' of the subject matter. And, over time, prune your haiku like a *bonsai* Master!

*

breath & haiku consciousness: the subtler realms
All forms of meditation and contemplation regard the
breath as one of the most immediate and potent
means for calming one's self, cultivating serenity, being
receptive to other forms of guidance, and having the
ability to be fully present in the moment.

The length of a haiku is said to be attributed to the
length of a breath.. or the time it takes to say a simple
phrase or have a simple exchange of conversation.

Considering that one "speaks" on the out-breath
(exhale), it is worth contemplating what occurs on the
in-breath, which is another way of saying 'inspiration,'
a word meaning "to breathe in spirit." Thus, if a haiku
can be spoken in One Breath (or really, one exhaled
breath), the other half is just as important, for it is the
silent place **before** the words are spoken.

There is also the place of "pause" that occurs after the
in-breath (or before the out-breath,) and before the in-
breath (or after the out breath). However you call it,
that "pause" is a powerful moment as well.

Upon reading a haiku, one is often transported to that
silent place or what can be meant by the phrase
"reading between the lines." The *kireji* "cutting-word"
within the poem reflects this.

And, upon reading haiku, one often 'gets' the meaning
right away, yet other times several readings (sometimes

over days, weeks, etc.) are needed.

*

personally
The haiku format can also be used purely for yourself and your personal path. There are some haiku that I don't show to anyone because they are so 'personal' (apply only to me and my path) that I wouldn't want, or care about, any response or comments from anyone. These, however, are of a different category than the haiku that I choose to share as an art form.

*

universal; guidance; mantra
One of my favorite 'haiku mantras' is from Soen Nakagawa Roshi, a modern Zen Master or *Roshi*.

AUTUMN (OCT. 8?) 1937

Bowing to Hakuin's Stupa at Ryutaku-ji in Mishima

Endless is my vow
under the azure sky
boundless autumn

(from *Endless Vow: The Zen Path of Soen Nakagawa, p.70.*)

I repeat this throughout the year, substituting the word "season" when it is not "autumn."

*

the haiku ideogram: a way or a voice..

through a tangle of vines

(original Chinese)

rén or **(jên)** + **fei**

kou or **chü**

(modern Chinese and Japanese kanji)

hai (Japanese)
or
rén + fei

ku (Japanese)

kou or **chü**

modern abbreviation

(The evolution of picture-writing for "man, person.")

*

Now here's what I consider the 'meat' of haiku, or if you are vegetarian the yolk of the egg, perhaps. Vegan are you.. how about the heart of the artichoke?

a voice through a tangle

"Thus Wu-men's comments on the various *koan* in the *Wu-men kuan* are intentionally misleading, the *koan* as a whole are called "wisteria vines" or "entanglements," and particular groups "cunning barriers" (*kikan*) and "hard to penetrate" (*nanto*). This is like encouraging the growth of a hedge by pruning, for obviously the basic intention is to help, but the Zen student does not really know Zen unless he finds it out for himself." (Alan Watts *The Way of Zen* p.163.)

"...for on the principle of extracting a thorn with a thorn Zen is extricating people from the tangle in which they find themselves from confusing words and ideas with reality." (Watts p.167.)

According to Susumu Takiguchi: "The word was not invented or coined by Masoaka Shiki as is widely believed. The word "haiku" had been in existence at least two hundred years before Shiki. What Shiki effectively did was to give this word a special role, that of replacing the "hokku" (opening stanza) in order to sever it from the rest of the renga ("haikai-no-renga" to be exact) and to make it a genre of modern "literature" in its own right."
> ("Sense of Humour - A Forgotten Prerequisite of Haiku"
> <http://www.haijinx.com/l-1/articles/takiguchi.html >
> 30 Oct. 2003.)

Even though classical *hokku* are often translated and called "haiku" today, a look at the pictographs of "hai" and "ku" (extracted from "haikai" and "hokku") will tell us much.

The pictographs provide a wealth of information, as well as adding new layers of depth, breadth and height to the true meaning and ongoing potential of "haiku." So, with that in mind, let's have a closer look.

One form of Japanese "picture-writing," called *kanji*, is derived from ancient Chinese; to decipher what haiku means 'literally' (or transliterally since Chinese and Japanese are picture-languages) we must look to the ancients as well as to the Japanese *kanji*. These languages also offer a clue as to the Asian mind. Although the modern forms are less pictoral, the pictures are 'imbedded' in the meanings, and the languages present a vastly different means of seeing and perceiving meanings than English's letters, words and phrases.

*

"**hai**" has generally been defined as "humorous, playful, sportive, or unusual." And "**ku**" as "sentence, phrase, stanza, verse."

The *hokku* was the starting-verse of longer "linked-verses" called *haikai-no-renga*, and a season-word was necessary to establish the framework for the rest of the poem. *Haikai-no-renga* were typically a literary party game that was played with various participants adding their own little "verse."

A haiku is thus: a single verse or phrase modeled after the *hokku*. Bashô is attributed with elevating what we now call haiku, to a more reflective, intuitive, and sublime level.

He did this by infusing the form with the flavorings of, specifically, Zen Buddhism and Chinese poetry, thus giving the form more depth and subtlety *along with* the playfulness.

But what is a haiku according to the "pictures" of the Chinese and Japanese languages?

Back to the pictograph (see pages 31-32):
In Japanese, **hai** means "actor" or "amusement" and is derived from 2 pictures:
  1) "a person" – Chinese **rén** or **(jên)**
  2) the idea/concept/abstraction of "not; non; no" – **fei**
     Thus, "non-person," hence "actor" and
     presumably, a form of "amusement."

From the Chinese:
"**fei**[4]: ...two sides, opposite each other. Abstract notion of opposition, contradiction, negation, wrong; no, not so." (Wieger p.337.)

Leaving aside moral issues of 'right and wrong' (which haiku makes a point to do,) and, instead, understanding "wrong" as 'a possible conflict', we get the gist of this as: "contradiction"; also, honoring "two sides"; and "negating" what doesn't work or is untrue, i.e. "not so".

With **hai** as "actor/actress," "all the world is a (poetic) stage," though in haiku world, more like a *Noh* drama with masks, where the emotion is felt, more so than shown.

The idea of haiku as an actor playing a role fits quite well with what many say that a haiku *is*. Harold G.

Henderson phrased it this way: "A haiku allows you to put yourself in the poet's place, and so to experience for yourself the circumstances that aroused his emotion." (*Haiku in English* p.72.)

Thus, one of the aims of the haiku poet is to allow the reader/audience to have a similar experience.

This is well and good. Yet, for **hai**, I venture another definition: "non-personal," or better yet: "impersonal".. not in an unfriendly sense, rather, 'lack of self-importance.' One of the qualities of haiku is that they paint word-pictures that do not accentuate or glorify the individual. Of course, many haiku have people in them, and even the Masters describe their personal experiences and insights, yet the emphasis is on presenting a moment or experience that is beyond self-aggrandizement or ego and reveals a connection of person&experience in a state of oneness. Taoism espouses this very same approach to life, for by accentuating the "impersonal" one is better able to transcend any pettiness or ego-based motivations.. and thus come to resemble the higher forces at work.

The actual pictures of "**hai**" are that of a person, plus the abstract concept of 'opposing or contradictory energies or things,' hence the "**non-, not, no**." This is another aspect of haiku: many of the poems present contrasting or contradictory images that, woven together, highlight the wonder and preciousness of life, the inherent unity of seemingly opposite forces.

"Zen and (European) poetry and haiku and senryu have all a sameness, in that two opposite things, or things of different categories are united in one. They all have a difference, in that it is different things that are united." (R.H. Blyth, *A History of Haiku: Volume One*, p.8.)

There are many other techniques along with "contrast," and resolving "contradiction". Whether the contrasts are 'opposite,' 'similar,' or 'related' in some way, well-written haiku tend to capture those moments of natural and dynamic 'tension' or 'ex-tension.'

"I was thinking then about what Kerouac and I thought about Haiku - two visual images, opposite poles, which are connected by a lightning in the mind. In other words, "Today's been a good day; let another fly come on the rice."(Issa.) Two disparate images, unconnected which the mind connects. ... I meant again if you place two images, two visual images side by side and let the mind connect them, the gap between the two images the lightning in the mind illuminates. It is the Sunyata (Buddhist term for blissful empty void) which can only be know(n) by living creatures."
(Allen Ginsberg. From a *New York Quarterly Craft* interview with Mr. Ginsberg, published in *The Craft of Poetry*, edited by William Packard, (Doubleday, 1974).)

Also, in a Zen way of speaking, haiku is what's left when you "not notice" everything else that is extraneous.

> steam fog dawn
> the yellow forsythia
> everything else gone

Although I wasn't in a 'problematic tangle,' this moment gave me clarity by reminding me that (along with the sheer beauty of this dawn moment) being-here-now is a state of heightened awareness, encouraging 'non-attachment' (as various Buddhists say) to material things and to the mere physical world. And that cannot be done if one is 'taking things personally.' Thus, **hai** can be interpreted as **impersonal.**

*

a voice through a tangle

The pictograph for **ku** "sentence, phrase" in Japanese, has "mouth" and "to wrap or envelop." Thus, "wrap one's lips or tongue around some words."

The original picture in Chinese is composed of *k'ôu* "mouth" + "*Chiu*[1]: ...intended to represent the tangle of creeping plants. By extension, curved, crooked, entangled." (Wieger, p. 145.)

And from that:
"Kou[1]: Curved, crooked, hook."
"Chü[4]: A sentence; because, in the Chinese composition, the end of each sentence, the pause, is indicated, when it is so, by a hook, which is the equivalent of

the European punctuation."   (Wieger p.145.)

Although *ku* can mean a generic "sentence," in the context of *haiku*, it transliterates from:
> "mouth – tangle of creeping plants" to
> > "a voice through a tangle."

As R.H. Blyth wrote:
> "...to clear away something that seems to stand between us and the real things which (in being not in fact separate from ourselves) are then perceived by self-knowledge."

Whatever the "tangle," and whether the haiku is purely about the natural world, humans, is serious, or humorous.. the 'haiku moment' frees the poet and the reader from the "tangle" of ordinary perception and, hopefully, helps the person return to a 'clear space.'

*

Wieger states "...in the Chinese composition, the end of each sentence, the pause, is indicated, when it is so, by a hook." What does a "hook" have to do with a sentence?

Interestingly, one of the traditional rules of haiku is that the poem must have what the Japanese call a **kireji** or **"cutting-word."** In Japanese these are not actually words of the poem, but a kind of marker or signal of where to 'pause' (a complex topic only touched on here). For English-haiku, I venture that the "cutting-word" is a specific word or place somewhere within the haiku, that acts as a pause, caesura, or punctuation informing the reader as such, often highlighting that particular 'moment' within the momentary-ness of a haiku. The haiku is split in two yet is a unified whole as well. In Japanese the **kireji** or **kire-ji** is said to occur after 5 "syllables" (really, "sound-symbols" or "character-sounds") or after 12. Thus, the end of the first or second line in English, though I find this to be flexible with modern English variations.

An example:

> no taller
> than the hedge
> a little boy

The word "hedge," or just after the word, would be the "cutting-word" or "cutting-place" here, as the pause prompts us to ask 'what is no taller than the hedge?'.. and then the little boy appears. Oftentimes, punctuation is used to tell the reader specifically where to pause.

Some schools of haiku may find punctuation heavy-handed, but it helps to delineate the haiku expression (in English,) thus keeping the images distinct and understandable. Again, the choice depends upon the individual haiku and what the poet chooses to accentuate or to leave subtly open to interpretation.

When writing haiku, however, I don't consciously try to put in a pause/cutting-word. (Similarly, one does not pay attention to one's breath when breathing 'naturally', yet one does pay attention when calming one's self, or while doing certain meditative or excercise techniques.) Only upon reading what I have written do I then see if there is such a natural pause, and if not, then see if the poem might be improved upon. The "cutting word" also helps to keep haiku from being a sentence, or merely one image, disguised in haiku form. Since most agree that a crucial element is the contrast or comparison of two images, the "cutting-word" helps to make this so.

*

reading between the lines
Although you may already do this instinctively, here's a suggestion for enhancing your appreciation of haiku.

To get more out of each haiku, or to get more into the haiku experience-- on the first, or better, the second reading, make a point to pause at either the punctuation or a natural break in the poem.. and you will have a fuller experience of the 'haiku moment.'

Notice the pauses.. what's happening there? Is the

poet giving you a clue.. or perhaps the space to have your own experience?

*

Looking or gazing at the pictographs (original and/or modern) serves as a "gate way" to the realm of Haiku Consciousness, Perception, and, ultimately, Expression.

Because of the "opposites" and looking at the middle-white-space, you will probably begin to notice more contrasting 'things' AND be able to find a **unifying** element. THIS becomes a "gateway" for "speaking through the tangle of opposites" and transcending dualisms— for that is what haiku do, at least according to the ancient Chinese ideogram.

If haiku truly are "impersonal," they sometimes touch upon what could be called 'god-speak,' or 'Spirit speaking through us in such moments.'

Overall, haiku can reveal the natural humor of life; reflect the immediacy of the natural world we call 'nature'; highlight moments or experiences of heightened, subtle or enlightened awareness, perception and insight; feature a specific time within a season; have a moment of pause or break within the overall haiku moment; and they are essentially:

impersonal (poetic) phrases
uttered with one breath..
a way through a tangle...

43

How one 'haikus' his or her way through a tangle can be done with beauty, simplicity, humor, and so on.

Some element of spiritual Zen-swordsmanship applies, as well, 'cutting-away' anything that keeps one from pure and unhindered attention to the natural flow of life!

*

a way through a tangle of vines
(transcending opposites/dualisms/duality)
People sometimes say "a snare in our plans" or "I'm in a bit of a tangle," "all tied up at the moment." Thus, haiku are more than poems, they are a tool or method for getting through difficulties and a means for appreciating life more.

One does not need to be in a tangle to write haiku, yet haiku express a 'clear path,' a 'window,' a 'doorway.'

From a Buddhist perspective Alan Watts wrote: "Therefore the practical discipline of the way of liberation is a progressive disentanglement of one's Self from every identification."(*The Way of Zen* pp. 37-38.)

In other words, liberation has to do with (or not do with) ANY limiting self-identifications. Before that though, one must admit to actually being in a tangle, and begin to identify the threads of such.

If one could imagine 'haiku moment' after 'haiku moment,' perhaps one would experience the natural high of life, the state of divine energy ever manifesting in such wondrous ways, breath by breath, moment by moment. Or perhaps, each haiku moment is best savored like a sip of brandy.. on lips, palate, throat.. and warming the belly and spirit of the Buddha within.

The often seen "ah!" or "!" or "..." is a method for conveying the sense of the un-conveyable.

Although haiku may not give us specific instructions as to our life-directions, they do give us models of a Zen-Buddhist and Taoist (plus others) way of observing and experiencing the world, and thus--
through our enlightened way of being, improve our life-directions, helping us to get through tangle after tangle.

*

the breath: overview
Although one could be partying and be so inspired to haiku, if we take into account the in-breath, pause, and out-breath of a haiku along with the haiku's 'inner pause,' we arrive at a kind of experiential and circular formula.

HAIKU originating from:
1) CALM and SILENT
   In-Breath
   Pause
   Out-Breath... Pause...

2) CREATING HAIKU
   In-Breath
   Pause
   Out-Breath (the spoken or written form)

   During the Out-Breath, the speaking, writing, or
   reading of a haiku:
   Phrase
   Pause (the 'hook')
   Phrase
   Pause

3) CALM and SILENT
   In-Breath
   Pause
   Out-Breath... and so on...

This gives a circular, reverential, contemplative, and
meditative approach to both the process of haiku
writing AND the speaking (or reading) of haiku.

Thus, these little poems are: haiku... one... breaths...

Part 2 - Haiku

1

utilizing the basic haiku format

(Let's see how all this works out with the actual expressions. I've adopted what I call the 'haiku format' to share three of the wise and pithy statements that I remember my father, Wally, often saying. Plus, there are a few more that don't quite fit the haiku literary genre. However, this format can be helpful for preserving such phrases and affirmations, and they do provide reminders of 'a voice through a tangle.' (Instead of a season-word, look for a "keyword" with, or without, a seasonal feeling.)

*

THE WORLD ACCORDING TO WALLY

Life is simple
but people make it
complicated.

(He trusted in the natural ability of life to take care of itself. This also reflects the "impersonal"ness of haiku and the Taoist sense of 'let life happen naturally, and all will be well.')

You'd better like yourself.
You're with yourself
24 hours a day.

(He wasn't advocating self-indulgence, rather, he was applying 'self like' because of a simple, inescapable fact.)

*

(Having no humor here would give an unfair picture of the man. Whenever Wally heard people, especially me, saying, "If only I had...," "If only this had worked..." he applied his logic and humor with a pithy (though perhaps not original) saying:

If your aunt had balls. . .
she'd be your uncle.

*

(The following is a haiku sequence by a 'granddaughter' Wally never met.)

Lunch with Saul and Mom

stories of Wally
go round table
smiles from ear to ear

he's just like the wind
can't see it
but i know he's there

at the end of lunch
the empty chair at the table
didn't feel so empty

— Ali Lebow (age 12)

*

The haiku format continued:

what wakes us up
is life and death, every
single one of us

*

the Beauty of You
in all of us
and shining outward

*

over 6 billion
on earth — how could you not be
a people person?

*

play the music
you still hear, after the music
stops playing

*

amor ahora,
y entonces amor mas,
todas las dias

love now,
and then love more
all the days

*

every moment is precious,
and suddenly there is only...
so much time

51

(Which is to say both:
 every moment is precious, and suddenly the
 realization of how fleeting time is
     as well as…
 every moment is precious, and suddenly the
 realization of how much more time can be
 experienced.)

*

even a cold man
has a green flower ready
to bloom from his heart

(Green is the color of the heart chakra or energy-center.)

*

con canción
en su corazón
todo es posible

with song
in your heart
all is possible

*

getting closer to "haiku"

-- for the Lebow family --

(written after the passing of a family member)

watering the earth
with tears for a loved one—
a flower blooms in heaven

*

far, far away
from the deer's thin legs—
war folk think berserk

(This one came to me in a dream after September 11, 2001.. reminding me to keep a place of "gentleness," like the deer, as well as reverence for the delicate balance of life.)

*

Buddha does not need
to say a word. Look!
the flower!

(During a talk to students, the Buddha was said to have twirled a flower in his hand. One student, Kasyapa, 'truly saw' and smiled, and was said to have received more of the teaching than any of the others who heard every word.)

'True' haiku give the reader a direct experience.. without trying to say too much.

spring

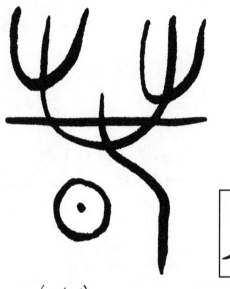

(ancient)

(modern)

The "Sun" is underneath the Germination of "Sprouts,
Shoots, Grasses, Plants." Sun-light gives the energy to
'crank,' or give existence to the Sprouts, etc., and they
Emerge (above the horizontal line — "the Earth")
to grow further.

Red-headed Woodpecker
rattles the roof's gutter—
first day of spring!

*

a group of robins
roadside on a patch of grass—
spring to the day

*

grackle's mating call —
white disk of sun appears
from the clouds

(The common grackle is a jay-sized bird that looks
all black yet has much iridescent color (bronze, green,
blue, purple) on the neck.

*

the "chip chip chip chip"
of the cardinal as April
snow begins

*

leanin' toward the sun
4" sunflower seedlings—
no-brainer

*

must be good friends,
three sparrows gathering
on a lilac branch

*

On the lumpy dust
of the path: a clean blue flake
of a robin's egg.

— Chris Clendenin

*

green pond   sheen of trees

three ducks' Vs of frothy white

geese preen   one swan   flight

— Vivina Ciolli
(This 5-7-5er shows how much you can pack into a
few lines: layers of rhyme; "concrete" image - "Vs";
use of spacing between words; alliteration; and lovely
overall imagery culminating rhythmically with the short
words/sounds of "one swan   flight".
This haiku was inspired by Roslyn Pond, Gerry Park.)

little boy
walking among the pigeons
all free spirits

-- Sheila Mardenfeld

*

rain on the windshield,
the wipers keeping time
to cool jazz

*

Hillside dressed in green
From evergreen to moss green
Spring

-- Kay J. Wight

soars above the stream,
then bluebird takes a breather
on a pine bough

-- Kay J. Wight

*

in the zen garden
sipping green tea
nibbling cannoli

-- Marilyn Riso Di Perna

(Along with the humor of mixed cultures here, the word
"nibbling" is used most effectively, and because haiku
are made of so few words, each one carries that much
more importance.)

*

quiet night
in the woods
caterpillars munching

--Marvin Schlesinger

*

When the toilet seat
becomes room temperature,
winter is behind us.

*

late spring evening
memory-knowing in the dark
where the light-switch is

3

summer

(ancient)   (modern)

A "Human Face," a "pair of Arms and Hands," and "a pair of Legs" with a 'line' through them to signify "walking leisurely." One interpretation is that the arms and hands, because they are held downward, symbolize 'hands of GIVING.' Another is that the arms and hands downward signify that the work of planting is done, and plant-life will grow of its own accord during summertime.

so still the tree,
and so then the air,
and so the heart

just cut summer grass...
i breathe in
twice as deeply

*

plain hot
or in prayer, people
on their front stoops

*

hot night
I toss and turn, fireflies blink bright
even the moon, too loud

— Victoria Twomey

down the path
to the garden
the sound of rain

-- Marvin Schlesinger

(Is someone walking there? Is this simply rain and
raindrops running down the path? The lack of
specifics highlights the experience of 'one-ness.')

*

Lightning ignites sky
Thunder roars in the distance
My spine slightly stirs

-- Yolanda Coulaz

*

new moon in summer
only fireflies
light the way

--Cliff Bleidner
(This exemplifies the heightened noticing of
'something' when another 'something' is not there.)

*

summer grass full of tiny fairies
riding fireflies—
ancient songs

-- Victoria Twomey

*

butterflies and bees
buzz around the snowball tree
not colliding

-- Cliff Bleidner

(An excellent example of the haiku pictograph at work,
for it is the "non-, no, not" quality that helps to accentuate the amazing natural harmony of nature and its
cohabitants.)

*

at the birdbath
a bee takes a tiny,
tiny sip

*

her bicycle
wobbles a bit today—
training wheels off

*

nothing much to do—
watching daisies
open

(These particular daisy-like flowers, called Gazania,
open and close with the sunlight.)

*

On a white pine stump
I count, with my penpoint, one
hundred eighty rings.

— Chris Clendenin

*

pouring rain
gushing down
outside the immovable home

*

Frisbees cut through clouds
Dogs rebound off amber sand
    Vision gently soars

-- Yolanda Coulaz

*

        Summer deluge.....
        golfers splashing on fairways
        and on greens.
                    -- Saul Waring

*

love the soft blue
twilight sky lingering on,
and on before dark

*

I cast my hook in a single stream,
God is love.

-- Russ Perry

(Russ writes:
"The "single stream" being an expression of 20 years
of metaphysical study, during which I examined every
"where" anyone could fish for "religious" truth. Some
decide to fish in many streams, some not even to go
fishing at all, but rather buy their fish from the market-
place. Mine became a single flowing stream...
God to me.")

autumn

(ancient)

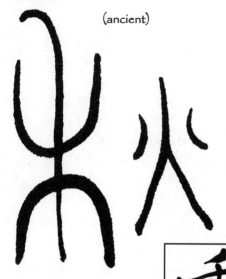

(modern)

(**ancient** - left half) A "Tree"
(branches up, roots down) with the
extended and bowed middle-line, signifies "Grains,
Cereals or Corn," the long middle-line being the literal
"weight of the crop" as well as symbolizing humility and
thankfulness for such abundance. "Fire" (right half):
flame with spark on both sides, or stick with two flames.

Fall is here

A squirrel's jaw

Stuffed with acorns

--Richard Savadsky

all the sunflowers
bowing to the earth
autumn rain

*

Wet, foggy forest shedding leaves
a crow's caw
echoes change

-- Richard Savadsky

*

Staid patience of trees,
and the little wild strawberries
dot the grass.

*

car window is down
and the heat on...
October drive

*

another lean
of autumn,
evergreen trees

*

Water crashing on rocks
Leaves falling silently
Peace

— Kay J. Wight

*

Las ojas son rojas,
naranja y amarilla
y tan fuerte como un hombre.

The leaves are red,
orange and yellow
and as strong as a man.

(After hours of raking, one gains respect for the combined 'strength' of leaves. This pushes the limit of
simile in haiku, and yet, gives a 'true' sense of the
experience.)

*

geese rising
over marsh grass
along rivers and shoreline

— Kay J. Wight

winter

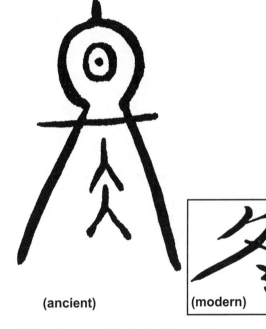

(ancient)

(modern)

A "Loop" at the "End of a Thread" is secured by a "Brooch or Tie" (horizontal line); within that loop is the "Sun," and below are "Ice Crystals." This "End of a Thread" is the end of a year when the "Sun" is contained. At Springtime, the emerging sun-light is contained again (below the roots,) yet assists the germination process.. as the entire cycle begins anew.

Where has the sun gone?
The dark moon has taken over

5:00 winter sky

-- Ali Lebow (age 10)

rainy afternoon
coffee lingers in the pot,
maybe snow soon...

*

Snow slides from a branch
Finches take flight
Vacant feeder

— Kay J. Wight

(Is the action -- snow sliding from a branch -- caused
by wind, melting, or an animal? The birds take flight
leaving an empty feeder.. swinging (though never
mentioned.)

*

After shoveling snow—
in the kitchen
eating vanilla ice cream.

*

snow storm
confined to the house
how delightful!

— Marilyn Riso Di Perna

*

cold night
the dog tucks in
and sighs

— Marilyn Riso Di Perna

*

Gray skies, bare branches.
Today i light the holiday lights
in my head.

*

the Arctic wind blows frosty cold
the little Arctic fox
goes with it

-- Cliff Bleidner

(Along with a lovely and palpable description, this portrays both a quality of Taoism and the philosophy of the Hopi Traditionalists: that of blending with one's environment and going with the flow.. not resisting the reality of the moment, but finding a way to 'get along' with that reality. The repetition of "Arctic" highlights this 'one-ness.' According to American Indian totems, the fox represents "invisibility," and this applies perfectly: white fox, white terrain, invisible wind.)

with accuracy
of a clock's second hand,
the icicle melts

*

open road
open window open mind
to mid-winter's day

*

Beneath frozen snow
vole, seed, hope sleep soundly
Spring waits her turn.

--Tammy Nuzzo-Morgan

*

two gulls
yellow-beaked yelps—
the mid-March snow

*

Icy rain.
Don't turn your back on me,
two days before spring.

*

in late winter
garlic tops sprout
green spikes toward spring

—Tom Stock

(Something perhaps only a garlic farmer would notice.)

一弓

seasonless haiku, or haiku for all seasons

This represents "Now," "The Actual Moment,"
and is made of two parts:

Three lines coming together   A symbol meaning
= "union" (a trinity, of sorts)   "contact"

Past, Present, and Future converging
at one "contact" point

is

"Eternal Now"

Paddling ashore in the still night,
only the heron sees me.

-- Russ Perry

*

half moon, one star
the river in the dark
a thousand voices flowing

-- Victoria Twomey

*

crows across
the dawn moon

*

we could not say
which is brighter, the light from
your eyes or the moon

*

waning light
and waxing heat, the threshold
where two seasons meet

(At summer solstice the days begin to get shorter (light-wise) though also hotter. Likewise, at winter solstice, the days begin to get longer, though colder, for which the poem would read):

waxing light
and waning heat, the threshold
where two seasons meet

(Could read as a couplet, yet "threshold" is accentuated.)

Looking up
away from the dry book—
rain drumming the roof !

*

such rain today
as never seen before...
familiar water

*

the brightest thing
on this grey rainy day
yellow taxi!

*

wet forest wood,
rushing water, reeds, rain,
wood-wind

*

stars
rocks
life

— Vivina Ciolli

*

even the gulls,
bowing
to this wind

*

after hot tea
children shuffling their feet
before the bus shows

*

Horse's big brown eyes...
and the moist, rugged world
is gentler

*

around the moon,
a veil of cloud
opens its curtain

*

raucous crows—
just above the horizon
a blazing sunrise

*

Circle of heat
Children of the universe...
Look up to you.

-- Sheila Mardenfeld
(This "circle of heat" could be the sun, or perhaps
 something else...)

*

shrouded by trees
beatific splintering orb
sunshine greets my eye

-- Christian Laura

*

In the changing
between day and night
a rainbow exits

-- Alan Semerdjian

*

wind swept the morning,
stars sparked the evening sky—
anything but boring

travelling here & there

(ancient)   **(modern)**

"To Go Out" from the image and idea of
'the second growth of the leaves of a plant.'

"Big place this world,"
he said, "yet look closely—
thin skein through all."

*

that's the kinda world
i live in, salmon going
up the creek

-- Brian Hassett

(This was spoken verbatim after I asked Brian (who
hails from Canada) if Canadian golfer, Mike Weir, is
a national hero. The question prompted his logical,
non-sequitur because one time while Brian was
watching the Canadian Open the cameraman
focused on a creek where salmon were swimming.)

*

going nowhere
pigeons preen, above
a gas station

*

Sitting in the car
Until we reach the airport
With nothing to do

    -- Ali Lebow (age 12)

*

                "life is grand
                even with a detour"
                say the trees

                      -- Alan Semerdjian

*

though not a dog
my left forearm enjoys the air
outside car window

*

highway divider   uncut grass gone to seed   tall yellow flowers

(Some feel that one long line, with space between
each phrase, has the flavor of the Japanese haiku
which are mostly written in one vertical line.)

*

strong scent, gas station—
first memories of travel
with Dad

*

Jeffrey's 13th Birthday (1-28-2002)

blurred lights
in the reservoir,
clear city night

(Haiku are typically untitled, the extra verbiage being
considered outside the haiku moment itself and a
literary crutch. In this case, the haiku stands by itself,
the title serving only as a personal reminder.)

Pine needles
on the solitary path
cry of a catbird

— Marvin Schlesinger

going upstate
the majestic mountains
going to jail

-- Cliff Bleidner

*

Jury Duty (4-30-2003)

after taking off
his old army belt buckle—
soundless metal detector

(This is titled to make the scenario clear.)

*

supermarket line—
granny buying cold beer
hard salami

*

rabbi walking
in the rain
keeps his head dry

(Having actually seen this, it was only afterwards that I
looked up the word and saw that a yarmulke has a
possible Turkish connection via *yagmurluk* "rain clothing"
from *yagmur* "rain.")

*

a bulldog,
an oriental man—
and the sidewalk holds us

*

for Uncle Alan
(1925-2001)

The seagulls squealed
and dove. You said you'd see
your father now.

*

so overcrowded
yet nobody's really there—
cemetery

*

- Keith's Birthday haiku -

wind and a freight train,
trees bend
above the campfire

*

her delicate expression
reflected in the glass
overrun by rain

— oliver ferrer fuentes

*

dome
of cool twilight blue, guiding
travelers home

*

after radio,
only wind, wheels, engine sounds—
rollin' home

*

underneath my feet
a piece of me is left,
after each footstep.

— oliver ferrer fuentes

home

(modern)

(ancient)

A "House, Room, or Shelter"
within which a person rests,
or a bird with wings backward
hence, landing back on earth.

*

so unassuming
this quiet gift ~ dusk, bells, voice
of a loved one

*

(ancient)   (modern)

Same essential meaning, except that here, a person is relaxing at home.. (turn pictograph counterclockwise 90 degrees, then compare with "person" on page 33.) The extended line is the "leg" stretched out.

*

Sun— low from the trees
brightens rice, water chestnuts,
carrot strips, snow peas

*

Purring fills my ears—
the bowl
licked clean.

-- Tammy Nuzzo-Morgan

*

smiling gold Labrador
with a sudden hollow belch
pleasure is complete

-- Christian Laura

*

Life is full
of little surprises,
pasta behind the stove.

*

the first drop of rain
hits my left thumb and misses
the cup of coffee

*

A chain-link fence
        divides our yards
                We still touch.

-- Ed Chemaly

*

the thin crackling
of the dry houseplant soil
being watered

*

this week—
watching skin of bananas,
ripen

(Simply noticing how something changes each day.)

*

cigarette smoke lifts
through rays of lamp lighting
following itself.

— oliver ferrer fuentes

*

tall plants growing
from rock crevices—
story of my life

*

gazing ...
the computer screen
through my wine glass

*

were i more bird-like,
crumbs beneath the toaster
would be my meal

一ラ

9

found haiku

(Poems 'found' verbatim or close to..
from unlikely or common places.)

tasting
of three apples
three ways

(from a dessert menu)

*

cup of fine grass
spider's silk, bark strips suspended
in fork, in tree levels

(A description of a warbling vireo's nest.)

*

marigold orange
the oriole's breast, rump, shoulder patch
...flute-like whistles

(May 26, 2004 - The color comparison led to the information. And whenever possible, I go for a "concrete poem" (which means that the physical shaping of the poem matches the words or theme). Only a semblance here of tail and overall shape, but that helps me to 'see the bird' whenever I read the poem.)
(Northern "Baltimore" Oriole from *National Audubon Society Field Guide to North American Birds: Eastern Region* Borzoi Book, Alfred A. Knopf, Inc. 1994 by Chanticleer Press, Inc./Random House, Inc. pp. 741-42.)

*

South Koreans throw
paper doves into the evening sky,
downtown Seoul

(from a news article, Spring 2003)

Oftentimes I find the wordings for haiku in letters
and e-mails that people send me when they are
describing images or experiences. After extracting and
shaping the haiku, I always ask them for permission to
use as such, and give them credit for the poem,
as I only served as editor.

10
haibun
(Prose followed by a haiku or tanka, and often used for
 travel journals.)

Had a springtime dinner in the city with two friends.
The delicious meal was followed by dessert with
green tea, the exquisite description of which on the
menu got me into haiku mode. After dinner, we
walked a few blocks. Looking to the west, toward
Central Park, between two far-reaching columns of
tall buildings— the bright glow of the sun diffusing
its light into the greying evening sky. The lazy after-
meal feeling was lifted to a place of gratitude for
such cosmic energy finding its way to us.. even on a
crowded, skyscrapered street. After parting with
friends and walking farther..

- for Willa & Saul -

heavenly green tea
and on this earth
brilliant sunshine

haiku and beyond: further possibilities

Haiku seem to me to be adaptable to a variety of circumstances, with perhaps even a genre of Sci-Fi-Haiku (or scifaiku as one website calls it - www.scifaiku.com). At first, one might shudder at the possible mention of technology and mechanical apparatus making its way into a traditionally nature-oriented poem, yet since Japan is well-known for technological advancements and a penchant for outerspace, consider the possibilities:

> night stars of Nephi —
> one of this space traveler's
> homes away from home

*

or a fantastical one:

> cobalt vegetables:
> this year's crops the bluest
> ever!

*

or love in the near future?

> there beneath
> Martian meteor showers
> two helmets touch

一 ラ

soft blu haiku (sensual or sexual)

> Ripe succulent plum
> You kiss me under its tree
> Juice sweetens my lips

-- Ellen Blickman

*

your legs, petals
thriving in the sun, dripping,
blossoming between.

-- oliver ferrer fuentes

*

shirtless, bronzed young men
landscaping:
    hot breeze

*

midnight oils,
the melting wax, moistness
from skin pores

*

after orgasm —
the refrigerator's hum
more and more distant

一ラ

Although one can playfully adapt the haiku format --
hikers (hike-ku); bikers (bike-ku); etc. -- retaining some
aspects of the traditional form makes for truer meta-
morphoses (or sub-categories) of genuine haiku, rather
than merely fanciful or mock-haiku.

*

haiku sequences & medleys

Now that we've explored haiku in depth, let's look at alternatives, along with other ways to apply the basic kernel of haiku.

As mentioned in the introduction, haiku are really an off-shoot of *haikai-no-renga* ("linked verse") originally long poems whose beginning haiku (originally *hokku*) eventually became what we now know as the 'solitary haiku.' The *haikai-no-renga* was a kind of creative chain-letter (or perhaps a prototype of the Internet and e-mail with 'link' after 'link' to different people,) a long poem that typically mentioned all four seasons.

Since haiku is a moment's essence, it makes perfect sense to string 'moments' together-- for that's what life does anyway!

Another format to experiment with is what's called a haiku sequence or medley: a series of haiku with one central topic is ideal for this. We'll also call this section:

haikai-no-renga (renku), haiku-ish, haiku-like, and beyond: adaptations to modern poetry (though closer to the original nature of haiku)

Since Haiku are too miniscule, non-descriptive, and unemotional for some writers, one way to employ haiku

into other forms is to write longer poems made of
haiku-like stanzas, paying less attention to many of the
technical specifics.

One can utilize the *haikai-no-renga* form of 3 lines /
2 lines / 3 etc. stanzas; or repeating *haiku* stanzas
of 3 / 3 / 3 / 3 etc.; or variations thereof.

> as good as the meal
> the warm smell in the room
> after eating

> And unexpected dear friends
> What special joy
> A gift without occasion

> — Saul Waring

(A spontaneous linked-verse. I wrote the first stanza,
and after having read it Saul added the second.)

*

The following were originally written as five separate
haiku, yet work together with a 'bird' theme. Yes, there
is supposed to be a "?" in the first stanza.

HAIKU MEDLEY

In the deep of night,
without making a sound–
birds prepare their songs?

        Dew
on dove feather
  on the grass,

lady cardinal's
orange beak takes the drab out
of a grey morning.

Must be good friends,
three sparrows gathering
    on a lilac branch,

four pitchers of water
to fill the birdbath. Shaking
    of wings and they fly.

*

sounds
Big Bang reverberations
in the conch

on the floor
a broken clay Buddha
still smiling

— Marilyn Riso Di Perna

(Cosmic time-lapse, cause and effect?)

(A spontaneous meeting with a couple of family friends, who also happen to have been recently married, plus the comment that sunflowers look "wild and happy," prompted the following haiku sequence.)

10 p.m.
on the city street, buying,
giving sunflowers

wedding present—
wild and happy sunflowers
at home in the vase

some day
the tiny seeds i planted...
tall, tall sunflowers

*

Years ago when I only dabbled with haiku, some poets and I called them "Ameri-ku." From our weekly poetry gatherings came the following (since revised).

3 Ameri-ku for Coffee and Dessert

auto-coffee drips...
clank of cups, saucers,
milk, sugar— chitchat

black stoneware filled
with Columbian. Steller's jays screech.
thank you, you're welcome

cups rise, tilt, banter
crunch, crumbs, slurps— next week
we'll do this again.

*

Quiet August Morning

in the still air
an orange-brown leaf
nosediving

backlit—
early sunlight
puts a glow to green and red coleus

amid the tangle of leaves
vegetables
hang down

green peppers
slowly
becoming yellow

remarkably
the thick cucumber
manages to hold on

>>

how some flowers
spill over the edges
of planters

like water rushing!
over a cliff
yet held in place

*

(With even longer poems, I pay much less attention to
whether each stanza is a *haiku* and whether there are
season-words and so forth. I simply find that a string of
haiku-like moments and phrases can make for longer
poems, though attention to such detail would give the
poems more of a *haikai-no-renga* quality.)

As If All That Happens Causes Ripples, Because As Far As i Know It Does

The lifting of the foot
from the gas pedal
at the precise moment.

There was enough hurry
already today. At the stop
light, i notice

a rabbit safely snacking
behind the fence dividing
the woods and road.

If you ever come out this way
there's a bump on Route 25,
and after that

may you have
smooth travels
to my door.

And if you don't come out this way
there are more roads than i know of what to tell you ~~
nonetheless

may you have
smooth travels
to some door

and may there be a warm smile
waiting there for you
upon opening,

or at least a warm feeling
if you live alone,
because if no one ever mentioned it before

God also lives alone
and in pairs and more combinations
than i know of what to tell you,

lives alone
as if all that happens causes ripples,
because as far as i know it does.

*

The following is a wonderful "haiku sequence" life-calendar in miniature by Cliff Bleidner. Each stanza uses a particular image or moment to express so much more.

Middlegrounds

in my mid fifties
all my favorite books
  falling apart

in my mid forties
climbing the stairs
  slower and slower

in my mid thirties
very drunk
  and very fearful

in my mid twenties
I eat my dinner
  then my dessert

in my mid teens
I break my mother's grasp
    for the last time

  at five years old
I discover the 19th street schoolyard
    "EUREKA!"

  4½ months in the womb
too dark
    to see my face

(There's a Zen *koan* that asks: "What was your face
before you were born?" This might be understood as
before being in the womb. Whatever the case, this last
stanza adds a wonderful balance to the previous
stanza and the poem as a whole.)

                    *

The following poem serves as a fine example of how
the 'haiku essence' can work in other formats.

SKIPPING STONES

i

sometimes, looking for the perfect flat stone
the face of a rainbow trout will break the river surface

ii

she had brown hair and the hands of an unwed librarian
whose face i have forgot in bakersfield

iii

a woman that pretty could skin a catfish on the american river
just by looking at it

iv

arm in arm we walked along the face of a crumbling white cliff
while mayflies danced over moving water

v

two fishermen in a passing rowboat and yellow rainhats
shouting angry instructions at each other

>>

vi

across the river a farmhouse with a rough horse pasture
and three white chickens in it

vii

so many ripe raspberries! when the sun came out
she took off her blouse and made a sling to carry them in

viii

after we made love her shadow lay quietly for a long time
beside an abandoned plum tree

ix

of course the money i loaned her ran out
she went back to oakland and that lawyer husband of hers

x

sometimes the sun is a rusty old coin
someone has thrown in the direction of san francisco
but missed

-- George Wallace

*

additional information
glossary:
Although haiku is influenced by various Asian mystical traditions, philosophies, religions, and art forms. R.H. Blyth lists the following 13 Zen flavors as "...some of the characteristics of the state of mind which the creation and appreciation of haiku demand." (my notes in parentheses):
1. Selflessness 2. Loneliness (in the sense of alone but not necessarily lonely) 3. Grateful acceptance 4. Wordlessness 5. Non-intellectuality 6.Contradictoriness 7. Humour 8. Freedom 9. Non-morality 10. Simplicity 11. Materiality (in the sense of 'not abstract') 12. Love 13. Courage. All are explained in detail in *Haiku - Volume One: Eastern Culture* (p.154 >)

some emotional flavors of Japanese haiku:
sabi; wabi; aware or *mono no aware; yugen*

haiku Masters:
* Matsuo Bashô (1644 - 1694)
* Kaga no Chiyo, also known as, Chiyo-jo, or Chiyo-ni (female) (1703 - 1775)
* Yosa Buson (1716 - 1783(4))
* Kobayashi Issa (1763 - 1826(27))
* Masaoka Shiki (1867 - 1902)

some haiku related art-forms:
haiga: calligraphy painting, illustration, photograph/ computer graphics (modern)-- accompanying a haiku and typically complementing the subject matter rather

than repeating it.

haibun: a page (more or less) of prose followed by a haiku or tanka. Used especially for (but not limited to) travel journals. Most well known is Bashô's *Narrow Road* or *Narrow Road to the Interior*

tanka: a distinct poetic form of 5 lines. (3 lines, plus 2 lines, traditionally 5 / 7 / 5 / 7 / 7. Numbers correspond to traditional Japanese 'sounds.') Can be written by one person or two: 5 / 7 / 5 & 7 / 7. Remember that you can write to strict form or adapt slightly.

chōka: long or epic poem

bibliography with notes:
(please note: there are numerous other reference books and many books, journals and websites featuring modern haiku (in English) that I have not read, but here's some information and notes on the ones I have read or looked through.)

HAIKU, TAO, ZEN...

Blyth, R.H., *HAIKU 4* Volumes *Eastern Culture; Spring; Summer-Autumn; Autumn-Winter.* Tokyo: The Hokuseido Press, 1949-52.
(Especially vol. 1, *Eastern Culture* for overview, history, and Zen-plus qualities of haiku. Distributed by Book East, PO Box 13352, Portland, OR 97213 - phone# (503)287-0974.
They have an excellent small catalogue of Eastern culture and haiku related books, including R.H. Blyth's *A History of Haiku* vols 1 & 2.)

(Blyth's 4 volumes of ~1300 pages, though naturally a bit pricey, is regarded as the greatest overview and explanation of haiku as stemming from the classical Japanese tradition. Although Blyth repeatedly makes reference to "religion" or "religiously," when what is truly called for is a distinction between that and "spirit" or "spirituality," these volumes have certainly awakened many to the variety and wonder of haiku both as an art form and as a reflection of its Asian roots.)

. Bowers, Faubion, editor. *The Classical Tradition of Haiku: An Anthology.* NY: Dover Publications, Inc., 1966.
(Excellent 3 page foreword with a concise explanation of haiku, plus wide selection of classical haiku poets. Very inexpensive.)

Gurga, Lee. *Haiku: A Poet's Guide.* Illinois: Modern Haiku Press, 2003. (Modern Haiku Box 68 Lincoln, IL 62656)
(Super guide with explanations, categorical listings, and tips on various types of haiku. Also many excellent modern poets mini-anthologized amid comments. Very practical suggestions on the inner workings of haiku as well as the overall spirit of the art.)

Hardy, Jackie. *HAIKU: Poetry Ancient & Modern.* Boston - Rutland, Vermont - Tokyo: Tuttle Publishing, 2002.
(Lovely color artwork along with a mix of classical and modern haiku arranged by Taoist elements "wood, fire, earth, metal, water.")

Hass, Robert, edited and with Verse Translations. *The Essential Haiku: Versions of Bashô, Buson, and Issa.* Hopewell, N.J.: The Ecco Press, 1994.
(Extensive notes, plus Bashô quotes.)

Henderson, Harold G., *Haiku in English.* Rutland, Vermont &

Tokyo, Japan: Charles E. Tuttle Company, 1967.
(Good basic introduction.)

Higginson, William J., with Penny Harter. *The Haiku Handbook: How to Write, Share, and Teach Haiku.* NY: Kodansha International, 1985.
(In-depth yet easy to understand introduction on topics both historical and modern. Higginson has also written numerous books on seasonal and other categories. Excellent for committed beginner, and of continuing value at any level. Carried by some public libraries. Well-regarded among haiku poets.)

Reichhold, Jane. *Writing and Enjoying Haiku: A Hands-on Guide.* Tokyo - New York - London: Kodansha International, 2002. (Her website <www.ahapoetry.com>)
(Lots of checklists, tips, techniques, editing suggestions, Japanese references, history.)

Ross, Bruce, ed., *Haiku Moment: An Anthology of Contemporary North American Haiku.* Boston - Rutland, Vermont - Tokyo: Charles E. Tuttle Company, Inc. 1993.
(Much nature imagery; wide variety of poets.)

Soen Nakagawa, compiled and translated by Kazuaki Tanahashi and Roko Sherry Chayat, presented with an Introduction by Eido T. Shimano. *Endless Vow: The Zen Path of Soen Nakagawa.* Boston & London, Shambhala Publications, Inc., 1996.
(Haiku and haibun from a Zen Master (Roshi), with introduction about his life and influence on the Western world. Excellent, especially for anyone who aspires to or lives a temple or monastic life, or even carries one's self as such amid busy daily life. His haiku have a multi-level quality that reflect his committed spiritual path or "endless vow.")

van den Heuvel, Cor, ed., *The Haiku Anthology: Haiku and Senryu in English.* NY - London: W.W. Norton & Company, 1999, 3rd ed.
(Provides "The Haiku Society of America Definitions." Variety of poets and styles; a mix of serious, humorous, and nature. Regarded as the original anthology of modern English haiku.)

Watts, Alan. *Cloud-Hidden, Whereabouts Unknown: A Mountain Journal.* NY: Vintage Books, A Division of Random House, 1968, 1974.
(Essays on Tao, tantra, reincarnation, modern topics, etc.)

Watts, Alan, with collaboration of Al Chung-Liang Hung. *TAO: The Watercourse Way.* NY: Pantheon Books, 1975.
(Not about haiku, yet has insights about Chinese calligraphy and superb explanations of Taoism and thus the nature and philosophy of Asian 'arts.')

Watts, Alan. *The Way of Zen.* NY: Vintage Spiritual Classics, Vintage Books, A Division of Random House, Inc., 1957, Pantheon Books Inc.; 1985, Mary Jane Watts.
(Wonderful book with historical and philosophical overview of Taoism, Buddhism, and Zen Buddhism with a section on haiku and the Zen arts, along with practical applications to one's life.)

Williams, Paul O., with Lee Gurga and Michael Dylan Welch, edited and introduced by. *The Nick of Time: Essays on Haiku Aesthetics.* Foster City, CA: Press Here, 2001.
(Reflective of the modern scene.)

Yasuda, Kenneth. *The Japanese Haiku: Its Essential Nature, History, and Possibilities in English.* Boston - Rutland, Vermont - Tokyo, Japan: Tuttle Publishing, 1957.
(In depth understanding of haiku and origins, with specific

guidelines for measuring each syllable and line meter, accents and un-accented; in-depth exploration of getting at the essence and spirit of haiku. A little more difficult to read but worth the time. This book helped me tremendously with achieving that 'state of being' from which haiku happens. Yasuda translates Japanese into English with 1st and 3rd line rhyme. While many frown on rhyme, I find that, occasionally, it makes the haiku easier to remember, like a favorite nursery rhyme (though the subject matter may not necessarily be childlike). Yasuda (Shôson) also titles the haiku, and calls his own haiku "Experiments In English.")

CHINESE and JAPANESE DICTIONARIES & CALLIGRAPHY

Fazzioli, Edoardo, with calligraphy by Rebecca Hon Ko. *Chinese Calligraphy - From Pictograph to Ideogram: The History of 214 Essential Chinese/Japanese Characters.* NY - London - Paris: Abbeville Press, 1986.

Go, Ping-gam. *Understanding Chinese Characters by their Ancestral Forms.* Third Edition, San Francisco/Larkspur: Simplex Publications,1995.

Rowley, Michael. *KANJI PICT-O-GRAPHIX: Over 1,000 Japanese Kanji and Kana Mnemonics.* Berkeley, CA: Stone Bridge Press, 1992.

Dr. L. Wieger, S.J., trans. into English by L. Davrout, S.J., *Chinese Characters: Their Origin, Etymology, History, Classification and Signification. A Thorough Study From Chinese Documents.* NY: Paragon Book Reprint Corp./ NY: Dover Publications, Inc., 1965 (1915 & 1927.)

INTERNET & WEBSITES on Haiku and Related Topics (a tiny sampling)

Gilbert, Richard, and Judy Yoneoka. "From 5-7-5 to 8-8-8: An Investigation of Japanese Haiku Metrics and Implications for English Haiku" Published in *Language Issues: Journal of the Foreign Language Education Center*.(2000). March, No.1. Prefectural University of Kumamoto, Kumamoto, Japan. <http://www.iyume.com/research/metrics/total2.html>

Kacian, Jim. "Beyond Kigo: Haiku in the Next Millennium" First Published in *In Due Season: Acorn Supplement #1* [2000] <http://www.iyume.com/kacian/beyondkigo.html>

Kacian, Jim. "First Thoughts -- A Haiku Primer" <http://blogs.law.harvard.edu/ethicalesq/stories/ storyReader$1352>

Khiron (Jerry C. Welch) the Kuei-Shen Hsien
WESTWARD-SINGING BIRD
A westward-transmittal of the Teachings of Lao Tzu's
THOU DEI JINN
and it's Chinese companion-classic "The Book Of Change"
YE JINN
<http://www.spirit-alembic.com/thou.html>

Marsh, George. Lessons for teachers and self-study <http://www.haiku.insouthsea.co.uk>

Natsuishi, Ban´ya. "Technique used in Modern Japanese Haiku: Vocabulary and Structure" <http://www.worldhaiku.net/archive/natsuishi1.html> (This essay from Japanese/English JAPANESE HAIKU 2001 (Modern Haiku Association, Tokyo, Japan, December 2000, ISBN 4-89709-336-8 C0092, 3,000 yen.))

Rosenstock, Gabriel. "A Haiku Path: Haiku Enlightenment,

Part 2" <http://www.worldhaikureview.org/2-
2/haikupath_rosenstock2.shtml>

Takiguchi, Susumu. "Sense of Humour – A Forgotten
Prerequisite of Haiku"
<http://www.haijinx.com/I-1/articles/takiguchi.html>

Yuasa, Nobuyuki. "Laughter in Japanese Haiku"
<http://www.haijinx.com/I-1/articles/yuasa-p1.html>
(from <http:// www.haijinx.com>)

"Buddhism"
<http://buddhism.about.com/library/weekly/aa020703a.htm>

"Haiku: theory and practice 'Counting Syllables' "
Designer and Webmaster: serge.tome@tempslibres.org
<www.tempslibres.org/tl/en/theo/mode04.html>

An Independent Journal of Haiku and Haiku Studies
<http://www.modernhaiku.org>

"A Message From Hoshino Takashi to the World Haiku Club"
(link to *World Haiku Review* publication)
<http://www.worldhaikureview.org/pages/whctakashi2.shtml>
(from <www.worldhaikureview.org>)

"The SciFaiku Manifesto" <http://www.scifaiku.com/what/>
Website created by Tom Brinck.

Variety of info. and poets <www.haikuhut.com>

Variety of definitions of haiku
<http://www.haikupoet.com/definitions.html>

*

author bio

Walter E. Harris III (known to poets and friends as **Mankh**) is a poet and essayist, and student of Kaballah. He has also published a modern epic poem, *Singing an Epic of Peace,* as well as three chapbooks of poetry, and has been studying Chinese calligraphy for seven years.

For more information on his activities, or to order more books, see page 142.

contributor bios

Cliff Bleidner -- Haiku poet, Formalist poet, Performance Poets Association™ Cofounder and Coordinator, retired Pharmaceutical Chemist.

Ellen Blickman -- founding member of the Galaxy Writers Group; member of The International Women's Writing Guild; award-winning member of Toastmasters International; Awarded the 2003 New Jersey Wordsmith Award for her poem, "The Unfaithful."

Ed Chemaly -- is an actor, director, writer, cook, and a student of meditation and the fine art of living.

Vivina Ciolli -- used *her* desk and desks in Writer's Colonies, to pen her poems and her chapbooks *Bitter Larder* and *Consolation Of Dreams*. She quilts, paints, photographs, sculpts, drums, and is crazy-in-love with her family of four cats.

Chris Clendenin -- his poems have appeared in *The Southern Review; Wascana Review; The Quarterly; College English; The American Poetry Review; Skanky Possum* and elsewhere. He lives in Green Mountain Falls, Colorado, and

Michigan's upper Peninsula.

Yolanda Coulaz -- poet since 2000, author of *Spirits and Oxygen* (Purple Sage Press), and photographer. Her work has been published, anthologized, and has won several awards.

Marilyn Riso Di Perna -- BA English; Published in: *Soundings* and Performance Poets Association *(PPA) Literary Review*; Poetry Group Leader specializing in working with nursing home residents with dementia; Long Island Alzheimer's Foundation (L.I.A.F.) Service Award Honoree.

oliver ferrer fuentes -- is twenty-five and lives in Brooklyn.

Brian Hassett -- has written for the *Village Voice*, *Rolling Stone* books, most major newspapers in his native Canada, and a funny how-to-live-as-a-temp book. He lives in an Impressionist painting with a Dalai Lama narration and Jerry Garcia soundtrack, and hikes tall waterfalls.

Christian Laura -- a native Long Islander with ever the mystic eye, he can currently be found in Huntington dividing time between his girlfriend, their turtle, and dear friends too numerous to list.

Ali Lebow -- is a poet and artist. She loves sports, movies and going to summer camp in Maine. She attends Trinity School in New York City, and loves to be with her friends. She became a bat mitzvah in June of 2004.

Sheila Mardenfeld -- CSW, MS. Ed. A Therapeutic Poet, her book *The Silent Poet Speaks* is forthcoming. She presented a training to clinicians, Using Poetry As A Therapy

Tool: A Proven Projective Technique. Performance Poets Association™ and Long Island Poetry Collective participant.

Tammy Nuzzo-Morgan -- has CD of poems: *Between Willows and Cedars*; haiku collection - *Fleeting*; and her first collection of poems *The Bitter The Sweet* (The Street Press, 2004) She is the founder and president of The North Sea Poetry Scene: <http://groups.msn.com/TheNorthSeaPoetryScene>

Russ Perry -- lives in Nissequogue, makes American country furniture and reproductions of Victorian-era toys, combs the beach, fishes, digs clams, paddles a kayak, and studies metaphysics. He is attempting to reconstruct his brain after two craniotomies. Also, the proud grandfather of four grandchildren.

Richard Savadsky -- former aerospace engineer; born in Brooklyn; father of three who live in New York, Orlando, and Denver; Performance Poets Association™ staff member; two cats, Magritte & Mirot; he enjoys poetry, music, and painting.

Marvin Schlesinger -- 61 year-old, single Jewish man; math and science tutor; hiker and lover of the outdoors.

Alan Semerdjian -- is a poet, artist, musician, artistic collaborator, and high school teacher. His website displaying his multi-talents is <www.alanarts.com>

Tom Stock -- had his first poem published in 1970 in Wetlands Magazine. 80 poems since; self-published 3 chapbooks; edited a fourth *Creations on Creation*. Hosts poetry parties in his home in Manorville, N.Y. Has a wide range of poetry subjects which includes the Pine Barrens.

Victoria Twomey -- poet and digital artist; lives in Huntington,

NY. Writing poetry since her teens but did not take the art seriously until the death of her mother in September of 2003. Two chapbooks published. Has been a featured poet at the Unitarian Fellowship in Huntington and on Radio Free Hampton's online radio show. Her work can be purchased at www.victoriatwomey.com.

George Wallace -- Suffolk County Poet Laureate, editor of *Poetrybay*, co-host of WUSB.org's Poetrybrook USA, and author of eight chapbooks of poetry. He studied Korean and Japanese poetry during his tenure as a Peace Corps Volunteer in South Korea 1977-79, and has traveled to Japan, Hong Kong, Thailand, Nepal, India - where he had an audience with the Dalai Lama - and to the Bamiyan Valley of Afghanistan.

Saul Waring -- retired Advertising person. Aspiring golfer. Member of unique pro-bono consultancy to non-profit charities. Neo-Haiku aficionado.

Kay J. Wight -- longtime friend and recent student of the author, she is improving her writing skills, and finds that by writing haiku she is more aware (via the senses) of nature. She is committed to learning more about haiku, poetry, and life in general.

*

publication acknowledgements

Cliff Bleidner
"the Arctic wind..."; "going upstate..."; "Middlegrounds"
(different version) published in *Soul Fountain* - Vol. #21
Summer 2004. "the Arctic wind..."; "going upstate..." publ. in
The Poet's Art. "new moon in summer..."; "butterflies and
bees..." publ. in *PPA Literary Review Vol. 8*.

Sheila Mardenfeld
"White footsteps—" publ. in *PPA Literary Review Vol. 8*.

Walter E. Harris III (Mankh)
Aside from select poems being published in my other books of
poetry, I am highly grateful to the following venues:
"Big place this world..." publ. in *d'Arts* - Summer 2004.
"plain hot... "; "supermarket line--"; "play the music..." publ. in
Soul Fountain - Vol. #21 Summer 2004.
"wind swept the morning..."; "tall plants growing..."; "were i
more bird-like,.." on <www.claritysight.com>
"far, far away..." with the title "Haiku for Innocence" on
<www.poetsagainstthewar.org> (6 Feb. 2003) and
<www.voicesinwartime.org> (6 Feb. 2003)
"were i more bird-like,.."; "rain on the windshield...";
"Big place this world..." publ. in *The Poet's Art*.
"Haiku Medley" - honorable mention, Performance Poets
Association™ 2002 contest; publ. in *PPA Literary Review
Vol. 7*.
"As If All That Happens Causes Ripples, Because As Far As i
Know It Does" - honorable mention Mid-Island Y JCC
2004 contest.

all day long this breeze
yet my mind is cluttered
without Your voice

*

inaudible
yet hearing Your voice
within

*

if being
in your body is not home—
where are you?

*

a place for your haiku, etc.

一テ